DK READERS

Level 1

A Day at Greenhill Farm
Truck Trouble
Tale of a Tadpole
Surprise Puppy!
Duckling Days
A Day at Seagull Beach
Whatever the Weather
Busy Buzzy Bee
Big Machines
Wild Baby Animals
A Bed for the Winter
Born to be a Butterfly
Dinosaur's Day
Feeding Time
Diving Dolphin
Rockets and Spaceships
My Cat's Secret
First Day at Gymnastics
A Trip to the Zoo
I Can Swim!
A Trip to the Library
A Trip to the Doctor
A Trip to the Dentist
I Want to be a Ballerina
Animal Hide and Seek
Submarines and Submersibles

Animals at Home
Let's Play Soccer
Homes Around the World
LEGO: Trouble at the Bridge
LEGO: Secret at Dolphin Bay
Star Wars: What is a Wookie?
Star Wars: Ready, Set, Podrace!
Star Wars: Luke Skywalker's Amazing Story
Star Wars Clone Wars: Watch Out for Jabba
    the Hutt!
Star Wars Clone Wars: Pirates... and Worse
Power Rangers: Jungle Fury: We are the
    Power Rangers
Lego Duplo: Around Town
Indiana Jones: Indy's Adventures
John Deere: Good Morning, Farm!
A Day in the Life of a Builder
A Day in the Life of a Dancer
A Day in the Life of a Firefighter
A Day in the Life of a Teacher
A Day in the Life of a Musician
A Day in the Life of a Doctor
A Day in the Life of a Police Officer
A Day in the Life of a TV Reporter
Gigantes de Hierro *en español*
Crías del mundo animal *en español*

Level 2

Dinosaur Dinners
Fire Fighter!
Bugs! Bugs! Bugs!
Slinky, Scaly Snakes!
Animal Hospital
The Little Ballerina
Munching, Crunching, Sniffing,
    and Snooping
The Secret Life of Trees
Winking, Blinking, Wiggling, and Waggling
Astronaut: Living in Space
Twisters!
Holiday! Celebration Days around the World
The Story of Pocahontas
Horse Show
Survivors: The Night the Titanic Sank
Eruption! The Story of Volcanoes
The Story of Columbus
Journey of a Humpback Whale
Amazing Buildings
Feathers, Flippers, and Feet
Outback Adventure: Australian Vacation
Sniffles, Sneezes, Hiccups, and Coughs
Ice Skating Stars
Let's Go Riding
I Want to Be a Gymnast

Starry Sky
Earth Smart: How to Take Care
    of the Environment
Water Everywhere
Telling Time
A Trip to the Theater
Journey of a Pioneer
Inauguration Day
Star Wars: Journey Through Space
Star Wars: A Queen's Diary
Star Wars: R2-D2 and Friends
Star Wars: Jedi in Training
Star Wars Clone Wars: Anakin in Action!
Star Wars Clone Wars: Stand Aside – Bounty
    Hunters!
WWE: John Cena
Spider-Man: Worst Enemies
Power Rangers: Great Adventures
Pokémon: Meet the Pokémon
Pokémon: Meet Ash!
Meet the X-Men
Indiana Jones: Traps and Snares
¡Insectos! *en español*
¡Bomberos! *en español*
La Historia de Pocahontas *en español*

A Note to Parents

DK READERS is a compelling program for beginning readers, designed in conjunction with leading literacy experts, including Dr. Linda Gambrell, Distinguished Professor of Education at Clemson University. Dr. Gambrell has served as President of the National Reading Conference, the College Reading Association, and the International Reading Association.

Beautiful illustrations and superb full-color photographs combine with engaging, easy-to-read stories to offer a fresh approach to each subject in the series. Each DK READER is guaranteed to capture a child's interest while developing his or her reading skills, general knowledge, and love of reading.

The five levels of DK READERS are aimed at different reading abilities, enabling you to choose the books that are exactly right for your child:

Pre-level 1: Learning to read
Level 1: Beginning to read
Level 2: Beginning to read alone
Level 3: Reading alone
Level 4: Proficient readers

The "normal" age at which a child begins to read can be anywhere from three to eight years old. Adult participation through the lower levels is very helpful for providing encouragement, discussing storylines, and sounding out unfamiliar words.

No matter which level you select, you can be sure that you are helping your child learn to read, then read to learn!

LONDON, NEW YORK, MUNICH,
MELBOURNE, AND DELHI

Editor Rachel Harrison
Art Editor Jane Horne
Senior Editor Linda Esposito
Senior Art Editor Diane Thistlethwaite
Production Editor Sean Daly
Picture Researcher Frances Vargo
Jacket Designer Natalie Godwin
Publishing Manager Bridget Giles

Natural History Consultant
Theresa Greenaway
Reading Consultant
Dr. Linda B. Gambrell Ph.D.

First American edition, 2000
This edition, 2010

10 11 12 13 14 10 9 8 7 6 5 4 3 2 1
Published in the United States by DK Publishing
375 Hudson Street, New York, New York 10014

DK books are available at special discounts when purchased in bulk
for sales promotions, premiums, fund-raising, or educational use.
For details, contact: DK Publishing Special Markets
375 Hudson Street, New York, New York 10014
SpecialSales@dk.com

A catalog record for this book is available
from the Library of Congress

ISBN: 978-0-7566-6281-3 (pb)
ISBN: 978-0-7566-6282-0 (plc)

Color reproduction by Colourscan, Singapore
Printed and bound in China by L. Rex Printing Co. Ltd.

The publisher would like to thank the following for
their kind permission to reproduce their photographs:
Key: a=above, c=center, b=below, l=left, r=right, t=top
Aquila: Michael Edwards 4 inset, Anthony Cooper 29t; **Bruce Coleman
Collection:** 4–5, 7b, 8, 9, 10t, 12–13, 16–17, 18–19, Andrew Purcell
14–15, Jane Burton 20, Kim Taylor 22–23; **Dorling Kindersley:** Colin
Keates 5 inset; **Natural History Photographic Agency:** E.A. Janes 11,
Stephen Dalton 21r; **Oxford Scientific Films:** J.S. & E.J. Woolmer 10b;
Premaphotos Wildlife: 25, Ken Preston-Mafham 29c; **Richard Revels:**
7t, 28–29; **RSPCA Photolibrary:** Jonathan Plant 6, E.A. Janes 30–31;
Windrush Photos: Dennis Green 24, Frank Blackburn 26–27
Jacket images: *Front:* naturepl.com: David Kjaer
All other images © Dorling Kindersley.
For further information see: www.dkimages.com

Discover more at
www.dk.com

DK READERS

BEGINNING
TO READ

1

Born to Be a Butterfly

Written by Karen Wallace

DK Publishing

A butterfly flits
from flower to flower.
Her red-striped wings
shine in the sun.

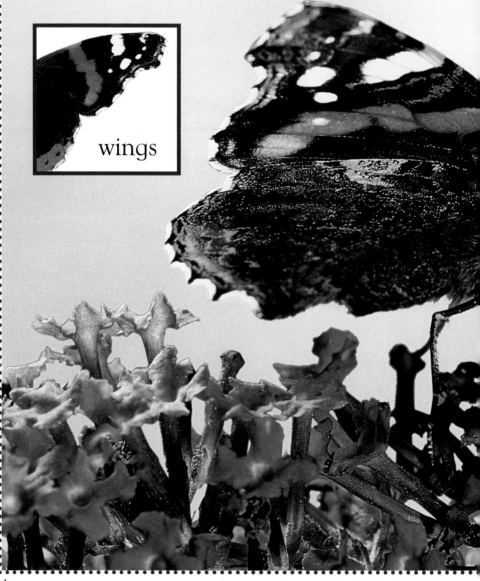

wings

She touches the petals
with her feet and her feelers.

feelers

She looks for a leaf
where she can lay
her eggs.

A butterfly flits
from leaf to leaf.

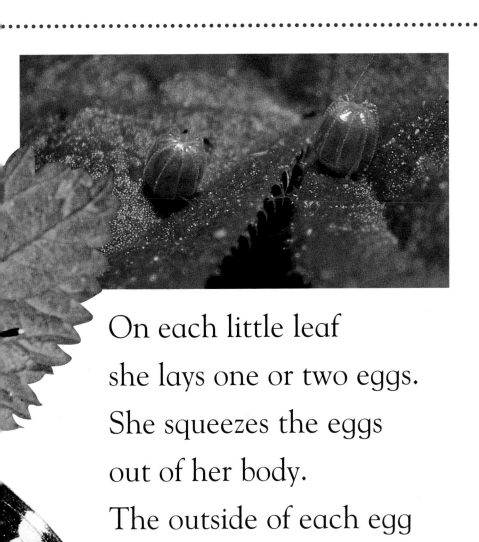

On each little leaf
she lays one or two eggs.
She squeezes the eggs
out of her body.
The outside of each egg
is covered with a shell.

shell

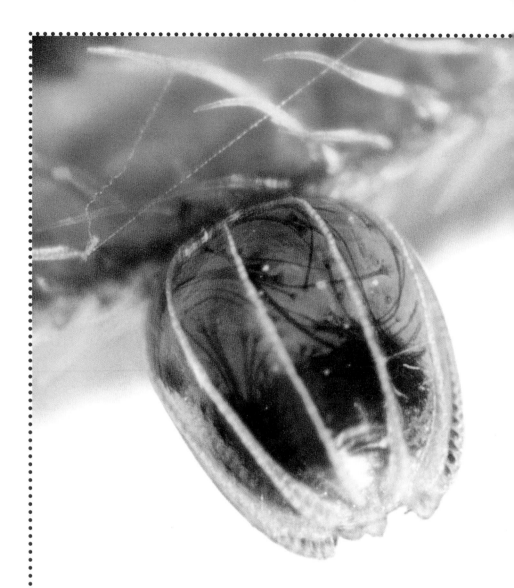

A caterpillar grows
inside each egg.
Soon one is ready
to hatch.

She bites through the shell
with her strong, sharp jaws.
She munches the leaves
around her.

The caterpillar makes
a tent from a leaf.

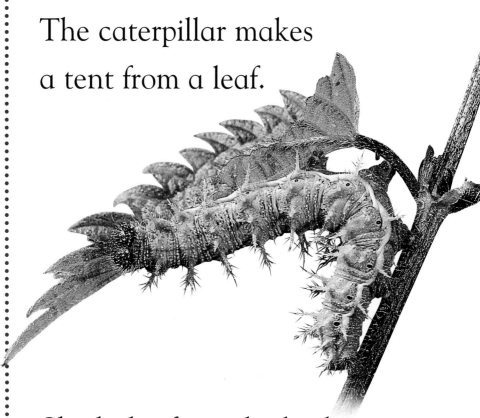

She hides from the birds,
who are sharp-eyed and hungry.

Hundreds of caterpillars
hatch alongside her.
Some are unlucky.
Hungry birds peck them.
Furry bats snatch them.
Spiders catch them.

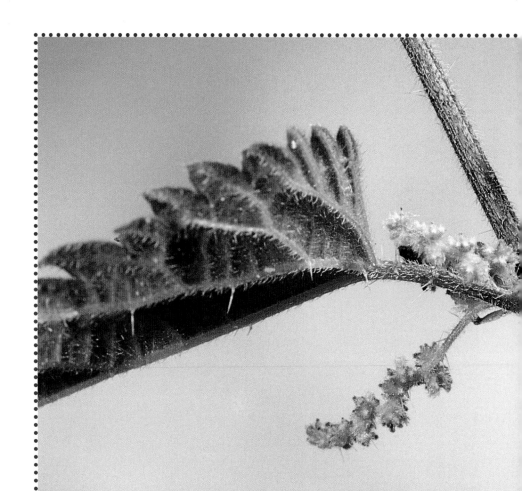

The caterpillar is hungry.
She needs to grow
so she crawls from her leaf tent.
She climbs up strong stems
and clings to young leaves.

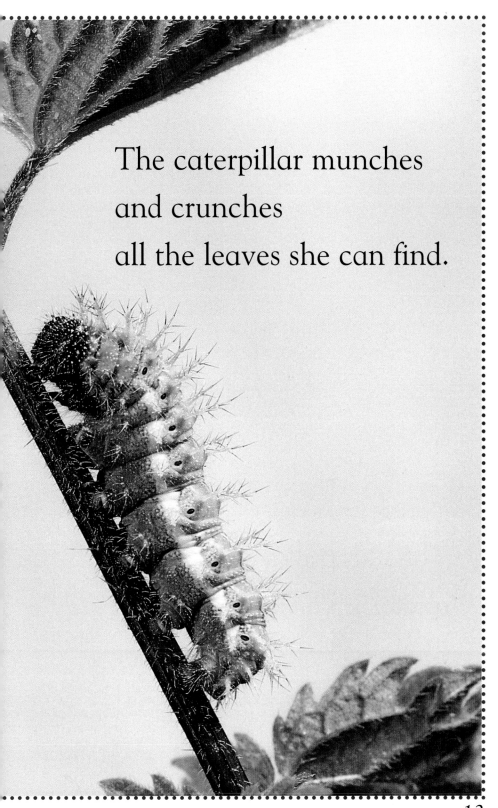

The caterpillar munches
and crunches
all the leaves she can find.

Munch!
Crunch!

The caterpillar munches
and crunches.
She gets bigger and bigger.
Her black and yellow skin
gets tighter and tighter.

skin

Suddenly the skin
starts to split open!
The caterpillar wriggles out
with a brand-new skin.

The caterpillar grows quickly.
She sheds her skin
four times
before she is fully grown.

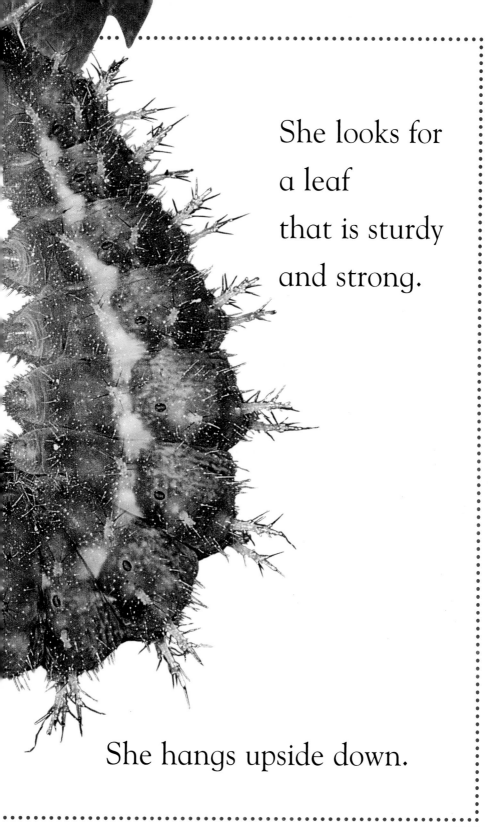

She looks for
a leaf
that is sturdy
and strong.

She hangs upside down.

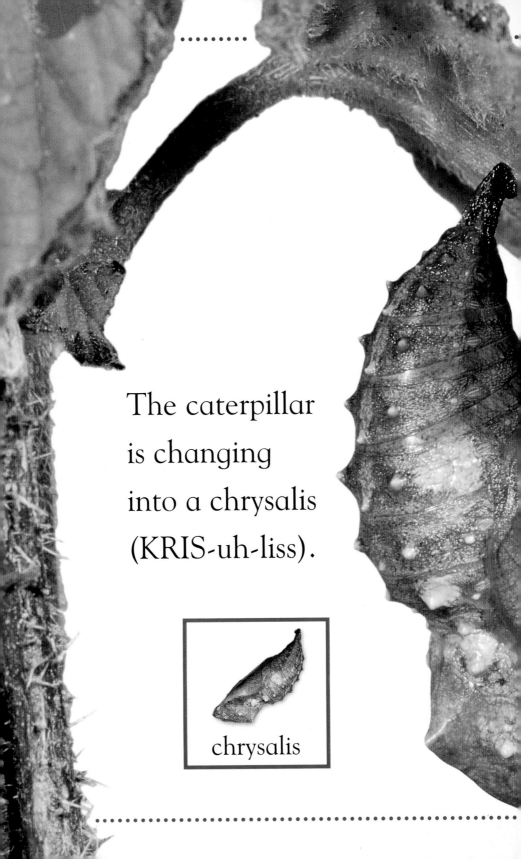

The caterpillar
is changing
into a chrysalis
(KRIS-uh-liss).

chrysalis

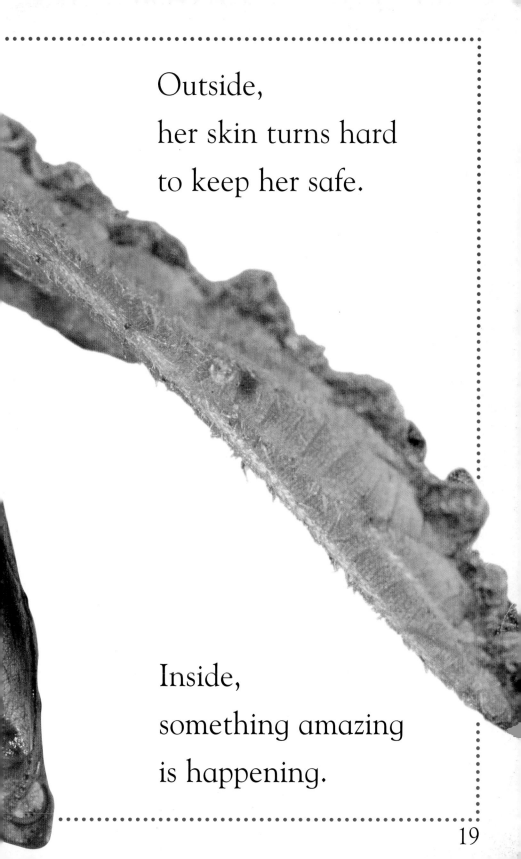

Outside,
her skin turns hard
to keep her safe.

Inside,
something amazing
is happening.

Then one day
the chrysalis splits open.
Something crawls out
into the sunshine.

It has a head and six legs.
It has wings and a body.
What can it be?

A brand-new butterfly
rests in the sunshine!
She is too wet to fly.

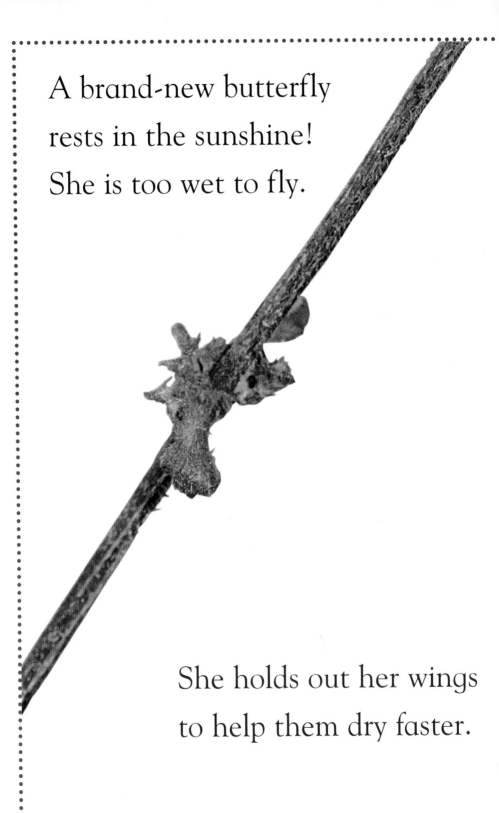

She holds out her wings
to help them dry faster.

The butterfly flits
from flower to flower.
She sucks up the sweet nectar
with her long, hollow tongue.
When she is not eating,
her tongue is curled
like a spring.

Sometimes she rests
with her wings held together.
She looks brown as the tree bark
so hungry birds can't see her.

Now it is time
to look for a mate.
She finds him
sitting on a leaf.

They dance
in the sunshine
and fly off together.

29

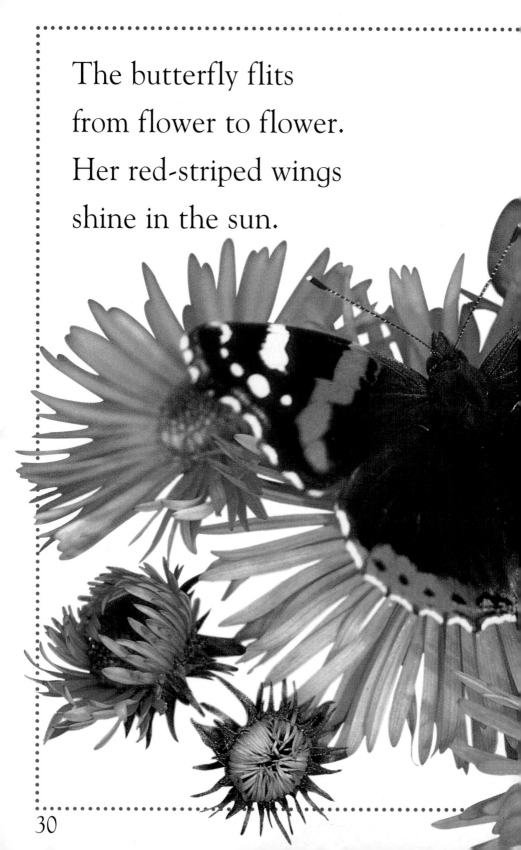

The butterfly flits
from flower to flower.
Her red-striped wings
shine in the sun.

She looks for a leaf
where she can lay her eggs.

Soon, a hundred
more butterflies
will fly in the sun.

Glossary

Chrysalis
the stage of growth from caterpillar to butterfly

Feelers
butterflies have feelers to touch their surroundings

Shell
the hard outside covering of an egg

Skin
the outside layer of a body

Wings
butterflies have wings for flying

Index

bark 27

bats 11

birds 10–11, 27

chrysalis 18, 21

eggs 5, 7–8, 31

feelers 5

flower 4, 24, 30

legs 21

nectar 24

petals 5

shell 7, 9

skin 14–16, 19

spiders 11

sun 4, 30–31

tongue 24

wings 4, 21–22, 27, 30